A Walk with Frank O'Hara

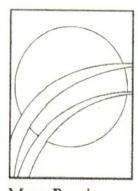

Mary Burritt
    Christiansen
Poetry Series

Mary Burritt Christiansen Poetry Series
HILDA RAZ, SERIES EDITOR

The Mary Burritt Christiansen Poetry Series publishes two to four books a year that engage and give voice to the realities of living, working, and experiencing the West and the Border as places and as metaphors. The purpose of the series is to expand access to, and the audience for, quality poetry, both single volumes and anthologies, that can be used for general reading as well as in classrooms.

Also available in the Mary Burritt Christiansen Poetry Series:

Unruly Tree: Poems by Leslie Ullman
Light of Wings: Poems by Sarah Kotchian
Trials and Tribulations of Dirty Shame, Oklahoma: And Other Prose Poems by Sy Hoahwah
A Guide to Tongue Tie Surgery: Poems by Tina Carlson
Point of Entry: Poems by Katherine DiBella Seluja
Victory Garden: Poems by Glenna Berry Horton Luschei
Suggest Paradise: Poems by Ray Gonzalez
Reflections through the Convex Mirror of Time / Reflexiones tras el Espejo Convexo del Tiempo: Poems in Remembrance of the Spanish Civil War / Poemas en Recuerdo de la Guerra Civil Española by E. A. Mares
The Gospel of Wildflowers and Weeds: Poems by Orlando Ricardo Menes
Walking Uphill at Noon: Poems by Jon Kelly Yenser

For additional titles in the Mary Burritt Christiansen Poetry Series, please visit unmpress.com.

A Walk with Frank O'Hara

Poems

Susan Aizenberg

UNIVERSITY OF NEW MEXICO PRESS | ALBUQUERQUE

ISBN 978-0-8263-6666-5 (paper)
ISBN 978-0-8263-6667-2 (ePub)

Library of Congress Control Number: 2024939084

Founded in 1889, the University of New Mexico sits on the
    traditional homelands of the Pueblo of Sandia. The original
    peoples of New Mexico—Pueblo, Navajo, and Apache—since time
    immemorial have deep connections to the land and have made
    significant contributions to the broader community statewide. We
    honor the land itself and those who remain stewards of this land
    throughout the generations and also acknowledge our committed
    relationship to Indigenous peoples. We gratefully recognize our
    history.

Cover illustration: Michael David, *The Judgement of the Moon and
    Stars*. Courtesy of Michael David.
Designed by Felicia Cedillos
Composed in Adobe Caslon Pro

for Avi, Isaac, Jonah, and Libby
—endless love

surely the strange beauty of the world

must somewhere rest on pure joy.

—LOUISE BOGAN

Contents

I

II

III

I

A Walk with Frank O'Hara

This morning I'm thinking of Frank O'Hara
strolling the streets of Manhattan,
debonair in white flannels, a small notebook
in one pocket, an egg and tomato
sandwich wrapped in wax paper in another.
He stops at a newsstand, plucks a *Times*
from the counter, buys a strong coffee.
Frank skims the headlines then takes his lunch
to Washington Square, a place I'd come
to know well a decade later, as a girl of fifteen
wearing beads and feathers in my long braid,
those days my friends and I patrolled
the Village, eager for Dylan sightings, careful
of the twitchy speed freaks panhandling
on the east side. These days I'd be lost
there as any tourist, gawking at the locals
and the new condos shadowing the avenues.
O'Hara sits on the same smooth rim
of the fountain where we'd perch to flirt
with strangers, giddy at cutting class. Unlike us,
Frank's urbane, *tres cool*, even as he sips his coffee,
chews his sandwich, and squints up at the sun.
Maybe he's considering which clubs to hit
tonight, or where to dine before catching
the new *Truffaut*. He opens his notebook
and writes his sure lines in an elegant hand.
Here there are no newsstands, and the shops

are closed, some for good, the streets
downtown deserted as an empty movie set
and as sad. I walk the bridge over the Iowa River,
wary, behind my mask, of those who come
too close. I'm trying to forget the morning's news—
the 200 at a house party in Beverly Hills,
the 250,000 riders in Sturgis. The virus
dirtying the air each time they laugh.
One writer warns that this is how we end,
not by contagion but because we no longer care
for each other. I stop and look out over
the river, imagine O'Hara and me walking
together in the city, and it's spring, and we can
smell the salted pretzels and boiled hot dogs
from the vendors' carts, the bright flowers
circling the plane trees. It's still the ugly fifties,
but the Kennedys, King, and Malcom X
are still alive, and neither one of us knows
anyone who's left *real life* for Vietnam.

Hunger

I used to think only of my father's anger.
Now I think of his loneliness.

—ROBIN BECKER

No fish, no poached chicken—
none of that *ghetto dreck*

he'd grown up on. For my father
my mother cooked only red meat,

rare steak and burgers, brisket and lamb,
hand-cut fries boiled in deep

bubbling oil, Idahoes the size of baby
shoes in their blackened skins—

all her life she planned her days
around timing those potatoes

for dinners served precisely at six—
the watery blood and congealing

globs of animal fat glimmering
on Melmac dishes she'd redeemed

her weekly green stamps for, a little dish
of iceberg dressed with Heinz

and Hellmans for salad. Unsatisfied,
he'd gorge all evening—chocolate kisses,

a family-sized Hershey bar, three scoops
of Breyer's, half-flats of cherries—

his anger the kindling that kept him thin.
Shameful, how I took my petty revenge

years later, serving him quinoa
and polenta with bitter dark greens

he could barely swallow.
I see him now, after work—

the dull office he hated, the long subway
ride from the city, the little money

and less respect he bore home—
our small black and white tuned

to Walter Cronkite or the Yankees,
a bowl of something sugary

and chilled resting on his flat stomach,
watching in silence, not a thing

to say to my mother or to us,
nothing from us he wanted to hear.

Sympathetic Magic

> It is not me myself I want to forgive
> but the girl I was who strode
>
> up . . .
>
> —GRACE SCHULMAN

Not to the ramp of a great ship,
but out of the ordinary

office of two divorce
lawyers and onto the leaf-

strewn autumn sidewalk,
morning sun from a child's

drawing smiling on her, she thought,
as only someone so young

can think, crisp winds cheerfully
blowing apart the raked-leaf

pyramids as if, it seemed,
the whole world—or at least

this quiet Connecticut town—
were celebrating with her.

She almost skipped past the quiet
brownstones, which seemed

to her happy, their windows
flung open to the clean

fall air, everything animated,
all of it designed to match—

like in a scene from some movie—
a musical!—if only she dared

sing—the way her heart felt free.
And when she pulled the ring

so easily from her left hand, she
wasn't thinking of those *sympathetic*

narratives on the cave walls
at Altamira she'd read about,

the fallen mastodons pierced
with arrows painted in berry juice,

a form of prayer for a good hunt
and to reassure the animal

of the hunters' mercy. And when
she dropped that ring into the sewer,

she stopped to listen to the *ssssh*,
ssssh of the water beneath

the street, and the joy she felt
made her want to run, and she was

not thinking of the *magic of objects*—
of Greek and Egyptian *poppets*—

nor of the thick bearskins some tribes
laid on the bellies of their infant

sons to make them strong men,
nor of the witches who knew

the *thing* could hurt the man. She didn't
mean to hurt the young husband

who had done her no harm,
except to be the man she hadn't

wanted to see he was, did not mean
to toss him away, though what

she did mean is lost now to the past,
the ring long since washed out

into the Hudson, and then to sea.

Song

So many lost afternoons, why
remember this one:

Tiny bells strung on white laces,
shoes with burnt-orange

saddles, bright April sun? A walk
beside a tall boy, his corduroy

jacket, marsh reeds bending
in the wind? Soft spring air—

April—that midday light
beside the reedy marsh, you

in your corduroy jacket,
me with bells
on my new saddle shoes—

Why remember this?

Why remember noon sun, a boy
in a jacket, a girl with bells

on her shoes—April sun,
reedy marsh, the boy, the girl—

of all the walks, why this one?
Silvery notes of the bells,

green smell of the marsh, a boy's
light jacket—those bells

singing in the wind. The girl,
the boy, that April sun.

The Beautiful American Word *Baby*

Once I wanted it growled low in the throat
by a Steve McQueen look-alike

as he pulled me down for a long, slow kiss—
me in my Liz Taylor satin slip,

him in his tight T-shirt and low-slung jeans.
Some steamy motel night. *Babe*

would do for more domestic moments—
Hey, Babe, have you got a second?—

not quite so good, but still clear as a ring
or my name tattooed on a bicep—

Keep away girls, taken. No *Sweetheart*, no *Sugar*
for my dream lover, too many

high-pitched consonants, too easy for salesclerks
and sarcasm, too Southern. Only *Baby*

sounded like whiskey and leather jackets,
the backs of Harleys, James Dean

and young Brando, pointy-toed boots
of worn-soft Spanish leather. *Honey*

was for drag queens and sitcom husbands—
campy as a big wig and falsies, homely as Schlitz

and socks on the bedroom floor. *Doll* reeked
of menace, cold eyes, hard slap, sharp

flick of a switchblade. *Dear* was unthinkable—
Ozzie and Harriet, virginal librarians

who hadn't yet transformed by taking off
their glasses and letting down their hair.

Baby it had to be, appreciative as a whistle
from the young hard hats in summer,

breeze ruffling a cotton skirt on bare legs.
Baby was dangerous, sexy *hitters*

perched on car hoods hot Coney Island nights
in July, signal clear as any other animal's

call. *Baby* was *I want you*, a warm hand
cupping a naked breast, a palm sliding

down a man's taut stomach. Musky sheets.
Quickened pulse. I was too young

to question—*Baby?* As in *child?* As in *mine?*
Not your Baby, reads the T-shirt

on the young woman I passed on the street
today, and of course she's right.

Even back then it was mostly a bad joke—
Who can remember every chick's name, man—

or habit, a tick, no more meaningful
than a pecked-cheek goodbye. Still, at sixteen

it seemed to me beautiful. Sleepy gray eyes
behind Ray Bans. A cocked cowboy hat.

There but for Fortune

Ah, but in such an ugly time, the true protest is beauty.

—PHIL OCHS

Not *Train*, your fevered brain's
manic incarnation, alter-

ego with his claw hammer
shoved in your belt, drunk all day

on orange juice and rum,
busting up chairs and mirrors

in the bars where *Phil* had been
so welcome. Not John Wayne, not Elvis,

not Audie Murphy, your unlikely
boyhood heroes. Not even

James Dean—your *Jim Dean of Indiana*—
whose nose you asked your surgeon

for, whose hair you modeled. And oh,
not that suffering ghost who

played for days that single song
on your sister's Far Rockaway piano

and then hanged himself
from a hook on her bathroom door.

It's the you that critics complained
was *never cool* I want to remember—

1969, and your almost unbearable
sweetness rising, a kind of prayer

from my bedroom turntable,
singing louder than the guns.

Eleanor Remembers Her Soldier

—1970

At twenty-three, Mike's the man, keeps a pistol
in his grandma's rusty Ford, holds whatever you need

in his basement stash. Six months home from Nam
he's still Marine muscled, has a bronze medal,

keeps his shades on in the dark. *Hey baby*,
he drawls when I walk in to Clancy's,

pats the stool beside him, courtly, orders me
a Sauterne. The wine's cold and grassy.

We don't talk much, lean into the jukebox
spinning Hank and Patsy till last call. Mike gets a six-

pack and a bottle of Wild Turkey, walks me home
to the shotgun rental I share with T, who's out

again. Black candles pool in saucers on the orange
crates, flicker shadows on Janis and the Doors.

⸺

We sit beneath Janis and the Doors, shadows flickering,
the bare mattress beside us with its question of who

or what we're willing to betray. Mike's got his back against
the wall, short legs stretched out. He's loaded

on whatever he's taken in the bathroom and drinking
from the bottle. *A firefight*, he says, his unit pinned down

so long in the mud and rain, *I just couldn't stay still,*
man. Ran across that burning field to Charlie's bunker

and opened up my M16—greased every fuck in there.
His voice is low and silky, and the room seems to shimmer.

I don't say a thing. I just want him to stop talking,
but he pulls his glasses down to make sure I'm listening,

and smiles and says, *It was a rush. I dug it—*
and now I'm a goddamn hero, got the star to prove it.

———

He smiles and says, *Man, if I did that here . . . over there*
and I'm a hero, got the goddamn star to prove it. The room's

become a cave, we're underwater, and he's not *Mike*,
not the gentle boy I like to brush up against, just a little,

the one who lets me blow on his cue for luck.
And though shame hasn't come for either of us yet,

something hovers in the dark between us. I want him gone.
And he does go, first draining the bottle, then

kissing the top of my head. Two days later, T and I
watch the morning sky flare and blacken over the draft board,

listen to the sirens shrill downtown, and we know.
Mike's run, rumors are to Canada. When the FBI

come, I think they look just like they do in the movies—
crew cuts and trench coats, shiny black shoes.

Eleanor Can't Sleep

so she puts in her earbuds,
listens to the old music—
here come old flat top—
remembers how T set the hard-cup
headphones big as baseballs
on her head, drew his shoebox
from its hiding place under the bed—pipe
and baggies, the lighter, the spoon—
tarry tang of opiated hash
harsh in her lungs, and then the slow
rocking, *shoot me*—
T's small square hands
on her naked back, warm circles,
skin and stubble—and now
the moonlight limns a green-gold
rectangle on her floor,
and she's seeing again the luminous
glow ball they tossed, giggling,
in the air, the arcing trails
tracing its flight—"was it an attraction
to darkness?" her friend has asked—
because the world is round it turns me on, because—
harpsichord and harmonies
the same now as then—and she
remembers—that falling away
of self into that "oneness"
she never found in prayer—

a variety of joy, ecstatic—
as once, on mescaline, she knelt
beside a toddler by a stream,
both of them absorbed in the glitter
of light on the water, the slick
cool of the rocks in their hands—
you never give me your money—
it was the lilt of bird song,
the heady perfume of apples,
and in T's room, the music
enclosing her, and always the splendor
of touch, the body, that rapt falling . . .

La Liseuse

This is the year the Eurydice sinks
    and the SS Byzantin. Here,
the World's Fair has opened,
    while back home the Senate debates

women's suffrage as the First Lady
    smiles and rolls pink and yellow-
striped Easter eggs across the lush
    White House lawns. Cassatt

does not show us the headlines,
    and we cannot tell from Lydia's
soft profile which stories she reads
    or what she thinks of them,

or that at forty-one she's just four years
    from her death, Bright's disease
already ravaging her kidneys,
    though neither she nor her not-yet-

famous sister knows this. They believe
    whatever ails her—the doctors
disagree—is in remission now,
    and so together with Mary she tours

the boulevards and galleries,
    attends the right plays and salons—
though she knows Mary brings her
    mostly as chaperone, to quiet

the gossips, and that she uses her,
    as a free model and housekeeper. It's Lydy
who shops and sews, keeps the accounts,
    stays the loneliness her sister

battles. Did she long for a husband
    and children? A lover? An art of her
own? Nothing survives of her letters,
    and little is said of her in Mary's,

except reports of her *devotion*
    and the family's praise. *Angel*
in the house, she's forever silent, her sister's
    Reader, her *Woman, Crocheting*.

In My Other Life My Mother Fails

to track down my gambler father in Reno, though as in our real life she
    tries every club
and casino, the hospital, the jailhouse, and SROs, and, too broke for train
    fare

back to Brooklyn, rents us a shabby room. To keep it simple, and with
    apologies
to my brother, in this life she's not pregnant. It's just us, alone in that
    city

as foreign to us as Madrid or Berlin. In my other life, she's still
    glamorous in stilettos
and fitted peplum suits, skirts short enough to flaunt her lovely legs, but
    not too short—

a girl without a husband has to take care. Each night before bed I help as
    she twists clean rags
into her thick, dark hair, and each morning I stand behind her, watching
    as she unrolls

a cascade of waves like Susan Hayward's. She paints her mouth blood red.
    She's well-equipped
for waiting tables in the casinos, makes good tips pretending to be sweet.
    She's lovely,

and the men all want her, but they like her loyalty to the jerk who's
    abandoned us,
and no, they've not seen him, but if they do . . . Let's say she leaves me
    with the kindly old dealer

who rooms downstairs, whose own gambling man has left her, too. Her
 name is Maisey
or Ruthie, she chain-smokes, wears a kerchief and housecoat, teaches me to
 cut the cards

as she does, and how not to be stupid when I play my hand, the right way
 to wear perfume.
Let's say I'm twelve in this life, pretty and not shy, that my mother starts to
 worry about me

growing up in that neon town with nothing but men and the desert
 surrounding us, and so she
 writes to her parents—in this life they're not hardscrabble immigrants
 from Ukraine, not a janitor

and cook—no, let's make them wealthy and here for generations, owners of
 a chain of discount
jewelry stores or a scrap-metal business. Of course they're angry at their
 only daughter

for running off with my father, who, as in our real life, is a handsome liar
 with little to offer
but good stories and bad luck. Let's say they relent and wire us tickets for
 the train back east.

In this other life we live with them in a three-story brownstone under lush
 trees on Bedford Park.
My Nana wears Chanel suits and white gloves, takes me to Bergdorfs for
 clothes, to the Plaza for tea

and little cakes, sandwiches with the crusts cut off. My mother pretends
 she's a widow, joins
the Junior League, sews bibs for the babies of the poor. At night she paints
 murky portraits

of my missing father among horses, dogs, and jockeys. In this life we don't
 live in the projects,
and he doesn't ride the subway home each night, clinging to a strap shaped
 like a noose, angry

and bored. I'm not homely or shy. I'm one of those neighbor girls who
 giggled at my
mismatched clothes and my plastic bag and my cheap shoes. In my other
 life it's me who's laughing.

Michael Corleone Prepares for Bed

Pacino's all weariness,
the scene domestic, a prelude
Coppola's framed to lull us,
a setup for the chaos
to come. Only a whisper
of far thunder foreshadows
the gunfire and shouting.
Alone for weeks and unable
to sleep, I watch the all-night
movie channel from my side
of the bed, a little light
from the hall seeping under
the door. Michael undresses
slowly, taking care
not to wake the sleeping Kay.
No *wise-guy* flash about him—
his suit is expensively
tailored, its pattern subtle,
his custom shirt white, pristine
as any banker's. And the scene's
not meant to be erotic,
but because you are gone
I'm seized with a longing so strong
I could raise a car with it.
Now Michael lifts tenderly
from his pillow the drawing
his boy's left him, and we know

in a moment the frenzied action
will begin, but I'm stalled here,
no longer watching, seeing
instead you, come home, the tired
way you'll loosen your own tie
and collar, undo slowly
your shirt, each button and cuff.

Western

—*LONESOME DOVE*

He's what we once thought we were,
the aging Ranger,

what we meant when we said *America*,
and when he smashes—

without warning or wasted motion,
his single move elegant

as Astaire or theoretical math—
the insolent bartender's face

against the bar and breaks his fat,
stupid nose, we're happy.

He should have shown some respect.
We like how he's sentimental

even when he's sober and not afraid
to weep over the young cowboy

he once was or the love he lost to his need
to ride on. And we like that he rode on.

We like the weary shake of his head
and the way he grins, a little sadly,

when he has to shoot yet another
savage fool. We like his tenderness

toward the broken girl he rescues,
how he kills her captors,

ten against one, and calls it fair odds.
He's what our fathers meant

when they taught us the lie
that only cowards are ever afraid.

We want to cling to him
the way the girl does, and we

like the way that, in the end, he chooses death
before he'll let the drunken sawbones

take his gangrenous leg, binds
his only friend to a quixotic promise,

and leaves his fortune to the girl.
It's for us she grieves, inconsolable
beside his coffin, for days.

Tea Boys

—*SALAAM, BOMBAY!*

Rain waters down
the milky, warm tea delivered
   to the district's young prostitutes

by dark-skinned boys
in white cotton. Barefoot
   and motherless, they believe

        at night the beckoning souls
of Bombay's dead children wander
     beneath the stone bridge

where, days, the living
gamble and smoke. *Baba the dealer*
     christens each

newly arrived *bumpkin*—
there is always a *Chillum*
     to smoke brown, to die,

       overdosed and icy,
trembling like a reed in the wind.
      There is always a twice-

abandoned *Chaipu*
still missing his mother—
        as if it's understood

    their old names
will be somehow wrong among
        these steaming alleys.

    Stacked tenements
crumble above the streets
  where they twist, too hungry

to sleep, these *tea boys*,
each one so thin, any slight arm
      could encircle him, though none does.

Jane County Corrections

The parking lot's enormous,
big enough to admit a stadium-full of fans
or a mall's worth of Christmas
shoppers, but no one here is cheering
or shopping as we cross
the frozen tar to the windowless jail,
Jane County Corrections—
corrections?—I carry
a brown paper sack like the ones
I'd packed your school lunches
in, but this one holds the public defender's
recommendations: toothbrush,
comb, a pack of Lucky Strikes.
It's Friday afternoon, too late for bail
until Monday—we're new at this.
The waiting room smells like a late-night
bus station, all of us crowded
on cheap plastic chairs, most of us
women, most of us black.
The woman working the counter
doesn't look up as she asks my name
and yours, tells me to sit.
We speak in whispers, and I think
of school libraries, study hall
where those of us who've misbehaved
must serve our *detention.* Time slows
until there you are, cuffed, in your orange

jumpsuit, shuffling off the elevator—
Is that right? Or am I seeing you
later, in that courtroom, where
in the stark light of ordinary grief
I watched you marched in by deputies,
guns on their hips, lined up
with the other petty thieves and addicts,
saw you look for me, then look away?
Memory fails, but I remember this
the way the near-drowned in winter
never forget the darkness and the ice,
your voice that night on the jailhouse phone
so like a boy's again, telling me
I had to come get you, you couldn't stay
there, you could *not be* in there,
the hollow sound of my reply.

Errata

What I took to be a slim wire
lost on the pavement
turned out to be a tiny snake
that whipped itself around
the panicked toe of my kindergarten
saddle shoe. What I believed
the smoke from a swallowed cigarette
burning in a young bully's belly
turned out to be only the mist
of his breath rising on the chilly air
of a foreign cold snap one rare
north-Miami morning. It turned out
to be a stone outside our window,
not a dead deer curled
beneath the oak, and that cry
through the bedroom wall
was not a hungry baby, but only
our neighbor's cat left too long alone.
That bite from some nasty bug
off the Smith Corona floor blackening
the skin beneath my jeans turned
out to be a third-shift splash
of the sulfuric acid it was my job
to dip the metal parts in,
and that closet I discovered,
jerry-rigged from textbooks,
around my son's third-grade desk,
a small prison his teacher'd built

to wall him off when he couldn't stop
talking out of turn. It wasn't a starburst
we saw that summer evening as we left
the theater, just a woman's sun-struck
hair. At first we'd thought it was snow
falling on the camps and trains
in the famous movie, those ashes
I learned were the words a friend
would speak one day, explaining to me
the transgressions of the Jews.
And what I thought the face of love
forever turned out to be heat
shimmering like water on a distant
blacktop, tar rising and then cracking
like my own lustful, fickle heart.

II

Charm against Recollection

Forgetting is, I think, a form of protection.

—DAISY JOHNSON

Forget the moon that night. Forget the sidewalk
   grates breathing steam, the stink and screech of iron
as the D train brakes. Forget the fraying curve

of the straps, those droopy *O*s held by our young
   fathers as they swayed, half-asleep, tunneling
home from "the office." Forget Jerusalem's

old city, the men in fur hats *davening,*
   foreheads pressed to the wall, the teenaged soldiers
sipping Turkish coffee in the sun, *Galils*

cradled on their knees. Forget that other sun,
   its light reflecting off Lolita's heart-shaped
glasses, Sue Lyon at fourteen projected

onto an enormous screen, the *ratcheta,*
   ratcheta of lawn sprinklers, her languid hip.
Forget the soap rainbow foaming your lover's

back and haunches in the shower, the golden
   rims around his pupils. Forget Dubuque Street,
the glassy Iowa River. And forget

the slaughterhouse stench, the I-80 exit
   to the cemetery on the other side.
Forget the dirt pelting pine coffins, the moan

of the caretaker's mower. Forget that space
   between the blinking cursor and the sad words
it hesitates before, and the one between

the edges of family photos and their frames.
   Forget the dancing astronauts, how they leapt,
boyish and giddy, to tag the virgin moon.

The Worn-Out Dancing Shoes

—BROTHERS GRIMM

Locked in every night
by their father, they escaped.
They dressed in silence,

—

in the dark, no sound
except the rustle of silks,
a single bright knock

—

against the trick bed,
its slow sinking as the door
opened and they passed

—

through it, going down
and down and down, as they do
in the Brothers Grimm,

—

to a shadow ball
beneath their palace, a world
beneath their dull world.

———

Each night the same tale
of descent and release, twelve
virgins escaping

———

the nursery, dull days
of French tutors and corsets,
off-key scales, and naps,

———

for secret forests,
a hidden boulevard lined
with gold-leafed trees, boats

———

shaped like swans, in them
twelve handsome princes waiting
to row them across

———

a lake so clear each
fish was wholly visible,
a starlit palace

———

where they danced beneath
hyaline light until dawn,
the slow return home.

———

What I dreamed wasn't
the palace or the lovely
and spellbound princes.

———

I wanted the heat
of their dancing, the music,
to know those wild hours

———

beguiling the nights
as if morning, its good-girl
rules and dailiness,

———

might never arrive.
I wanted my shoes worn through,
cool floor on bare skin.

This Morning My Friend Writes

to say the birds love her. *And why not,*
she says, *I keep the feeders full.*

The world is ugly. And the people are sad, I reply.

We know Stevens means to be ironic,
but I'm listening to the radio,

a BBC reporter recalling how, as the Taliban
rolled into Kabul, he'd watched as hundreds

clung to and fell from the enormous wheels
and nose of a US transport as it inched

across the tarmac. And because she keeps
no chickens, my friend continues,

she can welcome the fox, a vixen, she thinks,
who comes to her daily, *a ruddy shadow,*

white brushstroke of belly, darting in and out
of the tall maples bordering her wildflower-

strewn meadow—
        (*the fox*, I think, *is not a metaphor, the plane*
            is not a symbol)—

She says the birds love her, *and why not?*
I keep the feeders full. Tiny bright aerialists,

the hummingbirds tread the air beside her deck,
songbirds' chorus at her windows. She leaves,

she tells me, oranges each day for the orioles—*No
sooner do I put one out than they begin to work it.*

You're Snow White, I say, trying to be funny—
        (*the birds are not a metaphor*)—

But *the bear*, she says, *is another story*—
lately, she writes, he appears as the upended lid

of the barrel where she stores her birdseed
in the garage. As a five-fingered paw print

ashy on the backdoor screen. On the radio,
an Afghan writer's voice like a cracked recording

as he reports on town-square hangings, on hands
sliced off, girls sent home from school,

their mothers from work. In the photo my friend's
attached, the bear's head, a grainy shadow—
        (*immense behind the screen door,*
           a child's night terror)—

Poem Beginning with a Line from Louis Simpson

It's a classic American scene—
    1968, Jeannie and me sharing a smoke
        on the loading dock at the back

of the westside Target where we work
    the customer-service counter afternoons
        and evenings, my after-school job,

her *mad money* now that Duke,
    the husband whose name she's inked
        on her fringed purple bag, is over in Nam.

We're waiting for the fighters
    we know are about to fly over us
        on a training run from the base nearby.

Black lace and Emeraude, Jeannie says,
    watching the sky, *that's what men like.*
        I'm too young to know yet what men like,

but already I'm learning how loneliness
    drives us. Each break Jeannie tells me more
        of her life: how she first married

at sixteen, suffered three miscarriages
    by twenty-one—*I didn't get it,*
        she said, as if those numbers formed

some equation she'd been too dim
  to solve—how Duke's buddies watch over
    her now, alert to her laughter

in the bars downtown. Jeannie misses Duke,
  worries about her lover, a college kid
    she's counting on to split after graduation,

as they wait to hear his lottery number.
  The day is lovely, warm and sunny,
    and from the dock we can see the town's

golf-course greens, deer emerging
  from the bordering woods. Once, we saw
    an orange fox, but not today. And then

there they are, three jets in formation
  roaring above us. Jeannie grins and points
    as they disappear. *But they're our guys,*

she says when I say I hate these flyovers,
  imagine their cargo, fire, and blood. She grinds
    out her cigarette, says it's time to head in,

that next break she'll show me Duke's latest
  letter. *Only you* and *forever*—he signs
    each one in a round, childish hand.

Childhood

Those days my father had *had enough*
and disappeared for weeks,
my mother painted her nails scarlet,
said he'd be back *soon*. Those mornings
he was gone, I watched the bees
gathering pollen from our weedy patch,
their black-and-yellow fur bright
lures in the Brooklyn sun, imagining
our big Nash cruising among the distant
traffic humming on the Belt Parkway,
my father at the wheel, handsome
as a movie star or a hero in a book,
lit out for the territory like Huck Finn
in our favorite story. Those evenings
when he returned, after they argued,
the only sound was from the radio
until their bedroom door clicked shut.
In the morning they'd emerge
smiling like the wedding couple
in the living-room portrait, him skinny
in his Air Corps "pinks and greens,"
her a round-faced girl lost in yards
of ivory satin, a crown of daisies
pinned in her black hair. On our best
nights he'd take me walking along
the boardwalk at Coney Island, where
in the soft voice he used for stories

at bedtime he'd spin his litany of better
days, before I was born, when he flew
the Atlantic, navigating, he said, by the stars.
We'd rest on a splintering bench,
looking out at the dark ocean, listening
to the waves *shush, shushing* and the happy
screams and laughter of teenagers
around their bonfires in the sand below,
their voices rising to us in a language
neither one of us could speak.

Dish Pigs

Yes, it's just after dawn, stars still visible
in the slowly lightening sky,

but you're not like stars. And you're
not like the yellow dandelions

in the berm behind the reeking dumpster
where you lean, laughing

and smoking, on your break or shift's end.
You're not like the swift vee

of birds I can't identify shrieking
up into the morning air, or the children

in their little jackets who'll soon march
past us bearing *Frozen* and *Pokemon*

backpacks, though you're not much older
than the slick kids in their slick cars

who'll drive by headed to St. Pat's.
You might be the ex-juvie offenders

and dropouts I once knew there. Wiry
and muscled in your coarse aprons

splotched with grief—I mean grease—
cross-hatched imprints of hairnets

tattooing your foreheads, real tattoos
inked on your necks and arms,

you're the lowest of the kitchen castes.
The cooks and servers call you *dish pigs*.

It's what you call yourselves. I know
your skin is slick with fry oil, that the sour-

sponge smell in your hands lingers
even after you shower, that you know

the feel of thick rubber gloves deep
in your fingers. I know you take small

sacks of leftover burgers and fries home
to basement rooms where you play

Deathloop, get high, and dream. But these
are memories, fancies. Now the red

August sun's fully risen, and you call out
a welcome to the grayhead joining

your bright circle. You're not like the sun.
This is not *the yard*. It's just a strip-mall

parking lot, and you're not prisoners,
though you call the old man *lifer*.

only here. only now.

—LUCILLE CLIFTON

First think of a love story, a scene
in a '40s black-and-white film, strings
lush as perfume in the background.
We're in London, the nineteenth century.
Close-up on a woman's profile
framed by the small oval window
of a posh carriage, her fine-boned face
troubled through the etched glass.
The actress has dark hair, dark eyes.
She wears a satin dress, high-necked
and ruffled. She stares, but at what
we can't see. It's night, it's raining,
long rivulets gush down the wrought-iron
streetlamps, their lights blurred haloes.
She's waiting for someone she loves,
but she's not sure he'll come.
The camera pulls back, and now
we see it's his house she's watching,
that she's afraid to approach
and knock. He's played by a sober
Errol Flynn, or perhaps a young
Leslie Howard—slender, almost
female, a sensitive aristocrat, kind
to his inferiors and the help.
If he's married, he's tried to be good,

but his wife is of course terrible,
a shrew, or else she's sad and sickly,
clinging, her illness her own fault,
something she uses to hold him.
We've seen this movie before.
Voice over: we hear her thoughts—
only here. only now.—as she remembers
how he whispered those words to her
in a moonlit garden, or on a wind-
swept moor. Her voice is melodious
and low, as befits her carriage and dress,
the charming, darkened brownstones,
the sorrowful, sentimental rain.

Ode

He-who-came-forth was
it turned out
a man

—DENISE LEVERTOV

In those days we hardly saw you.
Pressed to talk, you frowned, suffered
our need in silence; but left alone,
you'd share sometimes a new taste
for *Beowulf* or quote Einstein's views
on war. Everything about you
seemed newly born: your widening
shoulders, muscles sculpting your
once-round arms, the deepening voice
I sometimes mistook for your father's,
all traces of childhood hardening
into those unmistakably male angles
and planes I have loved all my life.
We watched as you drove down
a basketball court, leather ball sure
as gravity beneath one hand,
the tall opposing guards gone
heavy-footed, you a jerseyed flash
between them, threading the key
for a sly reverse lay-up. We watched
as you lifted your first shovel

of earth into a new grave, your aunt
gone too young. *I don't want ever to die,*
you said, and we had no answer.
At seventeen you filled the house
with the echoes of your moving
on: slammed doors and long absences,
the insistent thrum of heavy metal
pulsing from the basement.

At the Chicago Art Institute

Past the flushed cheeks and hair ribbons
of the Renoir. Past the Seurat,

a clutch of small children cross-legged
on the rug before it, mid-tour,

the smiling doyen. *What is a study?*
Why are there so many naked people?

Past the Rembrandts and the two small
van Goghs I've never seen before—

La Berceuse, a woman rocking a cradle,
The Poet's Garden, for Gauguin—

Past the Picassos, I come alone upon *Suffering*.
Brancusi, 1907 reads the small gold plate.

Lit from above and below, the bronze
glows. It's a child, metal warmed

to the slender neck, the fragile wings
of his missing arms, the delicate mouth.

The child's eyes are shut, as if he's feverish,
the rims of his earlobes tender as flesh.

What moment's captured here? I think
of my friend, grown son sick

and without insurance, unable to work
or afford the medicine he needs.

I remember my own children's limp bodies,
how the heat of flu seemed to steam

off their skin when I touched my cheek
to theirs. Was this bronze child cared for,

eased into a cool bath by his mother?
Was he starving? Trapped in war?

Brancusi sculpted three of these,
the plaque informs, each head inclined,

like this one, as if the child were held
in deep sleep, metal made to seem supple

as skin glimmering beneath gallery lights.
I move as close as I can without touching,

incline my own head—who holds him?
Was his mother desperate for money,

offering up her boy's suffering for art?
Was he simply sleeping? *No*, say the tender

blades of his back, the arch of his slight
neck, the hairless, vulnerable skull.

From Her Chair in
a Hoop of Pale-Yellow Lamplight

my mother says my dead father is in his Heaven.
She believes for him it's a seamless blue sky

through which he navigates endlessly a cargo plane
like the ones he flew sixty years before.

He always said his war years were his happiest.
It's an old chair, covered in a faux-silk print

meant to look like French Provincial, a poor woman's
idea of *class*, the one in which for years she's rested.

Do you remember, I ask her, those nights Dad
wanted to show us how he could read, he said,

my ten-year-old mind—*think of a number*—
No, she says. Now she asks what I believe

happens after we die. My father's gone, I say,
as gone can be. No heaven, no hell. I don't tell her

I see him in the crooked back of an old man
pushing a cart at Target, in my own angry eyes

in the mirror. On those nights, I remind her,
you sat in this same chair, as this same yellow light

cast the rest of the room into shadow, watching
us on the couch. The numbers, I say, came swirling

out of the dark beneath my eyelids, white hot
as the center of a flickering candle flame,

and we waited, you and I, in silence for him
to call them. For him to tell us what I saw.

Shameeka

One generation past *island*,
Shameeka wears a heavy wig

of waist-length dreads,
hammered silver hoops

the size of small hotcakes.
She stands beside my mother

lying in her hospital bed and sings
Etta James a cappella—

At last my love has come along . . .

and this bedroom converted
to hospice use—my mother's queen

bed become a worktable
and storage space for diapers

and stacks of paperwork,
her doily-covered dresser top

now cluttered with narcotics
and syringes, the family photos

in their silver frames obscured
by boxes of plastic gloves

and the glass beakers
into which, three times a week,

the nurses drain toxic fluid
from her lungs—stills,

and there's only Shameeka's
soulful alto, the regular hiss-thump

of the oxygen machine,
and the sharp trill of Pablo

and Garbo, Mom's cockatoos,
singing along. Dust motes rise

like clouds on a pale shaft of Florida
sunlight piercing the morning's

shadows, and the room trembles,
as if it too might rise,

might lift us to that Paradise
Shameeka says awaits us.

Three Rispetti

1. Shift Reports: Skilled Care

Two weeks in, we get it: they have to show *skills*.
Dying's *not a skill*, but *uncontrolled pain* is.
We've learned to report she saw our dead father,
that she petted the imaginary dog
in her bed. That she begged us to let her walk
again. When she cries, *It's coming, it's dirty*,
and must be consoled as she wets the diapers
she's submitted to, that's *not a skill*. Neither

is the way we feed her now: sips of water
she sucks from a dropper, thickened applesauce
one teaspoon at a time. They don't need to know
the way she marveled at *all that equipment—*
the three wheelchairs, a walker, the leather lift
chair she'd refused at first but then admitted
worked *pretty good—for free!* And it's *not a skill*
that, bedbound now, she can't use them anymore.

Still, I can't help myself, must tell each new nurse
her story: this is brand new, she wasn't like
this—*See all these paintings on the walls? They're hers.
That's her unfinished canvas on the easel.
She lives alone. Flies all over. See how clean
this place is? All her. She's the designated
driver for her friends. She cooks, loves the opera,
film*—I still need to believe it might matter.

2. The Television

Until very near the end, it played and played.
Paternity Court, followed by *Judge Judy*
in the afternoon—*Fineh mentshn*, you'd say,
tsk-tsking and laughing at the unfaithful
men and small-time grifters, shaking your weak head
at this *crazy* new world. Nights, there were movies,
or docs on PBS, though you mostly missed
the endings, adrift on morphine and Xanax.

Only when you began in earnest the hard
work of your dying did it start to annoy.
The night nurse who could not stay awake complained
she had to have it on, though it startled you
from sleep, confused and afraid. We let her go.
M and I kept the volume low in the dim
study, the one room without hospice supplies,
our guilty oasis, except for the desk,

its deepening stacks of paperwork, sticky
notes, and the phone numbers of emergency.
Door cracked to hear you, we'd binge on *The Wire*,
grateful for the *hoppers* and *murder police*,
the ticking row houses and alleys become
a place where we could rest awhile in the pulse
of electric blue light. We'd watch till it lulled
us a little, until we could almost sleep.

3. Jag

It's the dying must be allowed
To mourn their own departing.

—OLIVIA MCCANNON

All day you'd ride morphine's black waves, not rousing
except once or twice, when you'd cry out, *That dog!*
There's your father! until evening, when you'd wake
and ask to eat, to sit up in the lift chair
in the dim light of your living room, the night
nurse exiled to the kitchen, your grandchildren
and me around you. We'd feed you applesauce,
a little mashed sweet potato, and you'd talk,

a fevered monologue, as if you were lit,
your poor brain's wiring overfired. Smiling
and laughing, a little wild, you'd go nonstop,
free-associating memories you'd revised
to shape a life pretty as a fairy tale—
your wedding story, the part where he left you
redacted, no three nights alone, no pawned ring.
A fable about your lost, favorite brother,

how as a child in Russia he'd killed a bear
with a wooden stake he'd carved. Pausing only
to accept a small taste from a spoon, or cough,
you'd go on for an hour or more—I confess

I timed you, afraid, and yes, annoyed, these jags
too familiar, these lovely lies you needed,
the played-out soundtrack of my childhood—me, blind
to what you were doing, what must be allowed.

Poem Beginning with a
Line from Adelia Prado

Once in a while God takes poetry away from me—
and then the silence is a barred door.

A boarded-up window nailed shut. That last gas
station for miles, *Gone Fishin'* scrawled

by the pumps, gage past *E*. It's the rockfall
that buries the pass, the drowned, single road

home. The angry beloved who won't answer
your text. It's the power out for days.

No matches, no candles, no batteries.
A busted flashlight. No voice on the radio

to companion you. No quicksilver shaft
of moonlight piercing the dark.

First Light

In the siren's wail
In the leaves' green trembling

In the rhythmic pounding
The workers make this morning

Building new houses up the block
In the sweet apple I eat

Dark coffee sputtering the pot
In my own heavy legs

Curled on this yellow couch
In the *Starry Night* throw

A fond student stitched for me
Another love I did not earn

In shovel scrape
In its echo, in the dirt

We scooped and dropped
Onto your grave

In sullen Florida sun
In my own death idling

At the station just ahead
In my beloved's chanting

A last prayer close to your ear
You come to me you come

Wasting, come sick, your skin
Like faded paper   you come

Smiling at the first light
Your face has known in weeks

In your leaving, in your hand
Cooling in my hand

People Knew How to Dress in the Forties

you always said, and here you are, lovely,
in this silent home movie filmed
by your older brother, your curly dark hair
chic in its snood, your tailored peplum
suit's flounce neat around your small hips,
every inch of you nineteen and dream-stricken.
And him, no wonder you believed.
Oh, movie-star handsome, blonde and slim,
green-eyed, that Air Corps uniform,
the leather flyer's jacket and silk scarf.
He came bearing orchids, and what could you
do but dance in your high platforms, giddy
with your first whiskey sours, your first
maraschinos, sickly sweet in the glass.

III

Monday

This morning it's the man lifting his bike
across the railroad tracks,

passing it up and over the chain link fence
like an awkward companion

and then riding off, a dark figure
heading toward the vanishing point

of the concrete canvas I fancy
St. Mary's parking lot's become.

It's in these gusts that ferry the weeds
and the three Target bags, blowsy

and transparent as jellyfish,
across the tracks and the deserted

lot behind him, and in the susurrus
of traffic rolling over the I-35 overpass,

where yesterday my student K drove
beneath the crooked legs of a man poised

to drop, the way a swimmer might
slip the pebbled edge of some suburban

pool. He didn't, *but still*, she writes,
she felt her life divide between the moment

his shadow fell across her windshield
and all the ones to follow. I think it must

have been in the voices of the cops who
coaxed him down, and in their pulsing

squad-car lights. In the eyes of the passersby.
I can feel it now, in the rising breeze

troubling the switchgrass and the chimes
strung from our porch. It's in the stray cat

making for the light and sound leaking
from our windows. In the robin, watching.

For Ruth Ellis,
Last Woman Hanged in England

—*DANCE WITH A STRANGER*

Your story is sordid, but still I can't stop
returning to it, to you trying so hard
to be like Marilyn Monroe with your red lips
and bleached hair, your skintight sweaters
and those fifties cat's-eye glasses
you would not often wear—*men don't make passes* . . .
one of those lessons you'd learned early
and too well. I watch again this film,
reread the clippings and biographies.
I'm more faithful than any of your lovers.
And how melodramatic it all seems—
the fading bar girl with a past, the pills
and booze, the men, the children
you couldn't care for. The spoiled
young heir who liked to race expensive
cars and had a taste for slumming.
The way you'd let him take you anywhere
he wanted—in the filthy toilet,
standing up behind the bar after closing,
in his car, the alley—how you liked that,
the way it made you feel desperately wanted,
dangerous, a *femme fatale* from the cinema.
How shut out in the cold London night,
watching his party behind yellow-lit windows,

the laughter loud enough for you to hear
on the street, you beat on the locked door,
shrieking until the cops arrived and gently
pulled you away. And that sad note you sent
his mother from your death-row cell,
a crude apology scrawled in crayon. I see you
as clearly as if I stood there, shivering
with you in the dark outside the cheerful pub,
waiting for him with the cold gun
in your small hand, wearing your glasses
this time, not wanting to miss. Not weeping
as you stood over him, but shooting again
and again. I can feel the relief flooding you
with such warmth it made you sleepy,
and you could finally rest.

Not One Woman
I Know Hasn't These Stories

I was eight, I was standing on a swing. I was glad
my little brother faced the other way.
I was twelve. I was on the bus, riding home
from the library. It was afternoon. It was raining.
I was fifteen. It was April. It was morning.
I was standing on the corner. I was waiting
to cross. I was daydreaming about the boy
from seventh period. He was on a bench. He was
watching. His pants were open, what I only
knew to call "his thing," when I told my mother,
in his hand. He was on the seat across from me.
He stopped his car and called me over.
How I startled. How I felt my heart. How I
needed to run. How I had to stay very still.
Not a bird nestled in the tent of his newspaper.
No puppy in his lap. The pale flesh straining.
The lowered page. No need for directions
when he rolled down his window. No one
seeing on the bus. No way to call back
the look on my face. His grin as he watched
me. His twitching eyes. His dirty hands.

On Reading That, According to the Jewish Calendar, Days Begin with Night

I think of my mother's Coconut Creek buddies,
all in their late eighties, clustered

around the condo pool in their floppy hats
and flowery one-piece suits

like so many withered blossoms. *Getting old ain't for sissies,*
they liked to warn. Meaning the obituaries

they scanned each morning on their sun-wrecked
lanais over bagels and decaf—*Who do we know?*

Who's younger? Older? Meaning the blue-and-white
ambulances, ubiquitous as the surrey-fringed

golf carts prowling their *planned community,*
screaming harbingers among the rapacious

tropical blooms and subdued fake lawns. Meaning
walkers, nurses, and *companions* from the islands.

Meaning hip fractures, glaucoma. Tumors. Each new
day not a beginning, but one day less. At sixty-nine,

you and I are *babies,* they scoff, but hasn't it begun?
This one surprises his wife with new hearing aids

in lieu of birthday roses. That one's darling needs
new medications for his fragile heart. Gray hair,

less hair, lost reading glasses. Vanity's the least of it.
Making love's acrobatic, but not in some up-

against-the-elevator-wall Cinemax way. And of course,
it's an illusion, and no work for the sun, what we call

its *rising* and *setting*, as we turn and turn, passing
in and out of its light. Night doesn't fall,

day does not break. It's this fragile earth, endlessly
circling and spinning, that we should pity.

Now That You're Nowhere

anyone on earth can find you,
I find you here,

in age-softened envelopes
postmarked *Par Avion,*

San Francisco, 1959,
hidden at the back

of my mother's closet
beneath stacks of frayed

linens. *Goddess*, you write,
I was stunned to find

you'd changed the locks.
Now that you're nothing

but black ink, your familiar
hand elegant, precise,

at first, as printer's type,
then falling apart,

as you did, toward the end
of each letter, growing

larger, loopy, spilling down
the pages, you're these words

I shouldn't read, but do:
you're *hungry* and *ill*,

casino, motel. You're *jail.*
You're *poison in the glove box,*

shirts and ties she took.
You're *sorrow* and *sorry.*

You're *rage. I never knew,*
you write, *you hated me so much*

you couldn't bear to leave
me even my razor. Please don't

write me anymore about my
children. Check soon.

Blackhawk Park

It's summer, and the kids are out of school and here,
　　at this spongy-surfaced playground with their mothers
and their day-care minders, along with those of us—
　　mostly academics or the self-employed—free
to come sit in the park on this weekday morning.
　　The children shout and wrestle, play tag, hang upside-

down on braided ladders. It's a mild, sunny day,
　　and we're easy in our skins, unafraid to doze
or read, here on these cheerfully painted benches.
　　Signs etched on the corner shop's window exhort us:
Create! Collaborate! Be Inclusive! but lulled
　　by these mild breezes off the prairie, we're content

to drift in our separate reveries. Up the block,
　　a yellow crane lifts its load of bricks to the roof
of the new Hampton Inn, its *beep-beep-beep* merging
　　with the sounds of a small plane passing overhead,
sparrows singing, the children's shrieks and laughter. Then—
　　another sound—a man and woman's rough voices

piercing the air as they round the corner shouting,
　　a couple in their fifties wearing leather vests
too heavy for the season, she with razor-cut,
　　hennaed hair, a bald eagle's spread wings inked across
her freckled chest, he with a red bandanna tied
　　around his shaved head, chain bracelets on both wrists, cut-

off jeans, *River City Riders* spelled out in studs
    on their backs, their loud argument like a racket
of crows come suddenly among us. We're working
    hard not to get caught watching—the mothers stepping
to their children, tying knotted laces, wiping
    dry noses; the man beside me deep in his phone,

me in my book—as we calculate our options:
    intervene? call the cops? And then they get quiet,
their faces close, and she shoves him, hard. He stumbles,
    then rights himself, shoves her softly back. She's crying
now, and as he pulls her to him, you can almost
    hear us chorus our exhalations, our relief

palpable as the wind that's picked up to shiver
    the full leaves of the oaks. Arms around each other,
the couple crosses out of the playground. The sun
    grows hotter, the children protesting as they're called
to juice and sandwiches in the shade. Downriver,
    the abandoned ironworks shrills its noon whistle.

Postcard from New Hampshire

Driving backcountry roads, we watch
for storms, remembering that here in the Valley

downhill always leads home. Black birches
and the hammered nickel of the river

gleam in late-afternoon sun then vanish
into lusher forest, the saturated greens

of trees thick with weeks of rain.
Beside the now-scenic mill converting

to condos, the falls are picturesque.
Inside, new windows etched to look old

and fresh brick lining the cracked walls
bear the gone coughs of the dead

mill workers and their great-grandchildren,
who drink too much, work the season,

must collect unemployment all winter.
Today, we park among the pickups

with For Sale signs ringing the lake,
spread our Sunday picnic by the shore.

Reflected in its blue waters, the sky's gone
suburban as a backyard pool.

These towering clouds appear to sink
into it, tangible as trap rock.

Autobiographobia

> I have a disease called autobiographobia.
>
> —CHEKHOV

I am the orphan, wrenched like a slight arm
from its socket, from my life of privilege.

I am the rough girl with a tall beehive
and white lips, beloved of *Teddy boys*,

feral on rooftops rife with new mysteries
of cigarettes and sex. I have walked

shivering strands of metal thousands of feet
above the pavement, thrilling the open-

mouthed crowds below, their heads tilted like birds
waiting to be fed the food of my death,

and I am the way his lover trembled,
even thirty years later, remembering

how those wires sang. I am the last woman
hanged in England for killing a careless,

beautiful boy I could not stop wanting,
and I am his mother and the crayoned

scrawl of the Death Row note she refuses
to read. I am the fugitive rebel

underground in plain sight and the blind whine
of her husband's suburban mower. I'm

that sweet wind that luffs their sheets waving *hi*
on the line, the slow roll across gravel

of the agents' tires when they come for her.
I'm the story they will want her to tell.

On Your Wedding Day,
You Must Fast And Weep

A Found Poem

so that the evil spirits believe you
are in mourning and feel no need to curse
   your union. Don't marry on Monday,
which is not mentioned in the Torah.

   Before your groom can step on your toes
in your satin slipper beneath the *chuppa*,
   bring your heel down, hard, on his heavy shoe,
and you will rule your home forever.

   When it's your time of the month, do not bake:
your cakes won't rise. Do not make soup,
   which will not keep. Your plants will blacken
and die if you water them. To spark passion

   in your husband, serve him fish on Friday
nights. When the child arrives,
   do not cut his hair before he speaks, or
he'll stay silent. Don't kiss him too much,

   or the roses will fade from his cheeks.
If your girl laughs in her sleep she's at play
   with the Angel of Death. If she falls ill,
if she is dying, pretend to sell her for a *sheckel*,

and she may live. Hang garlic and onions
on every door and window in times of epidemic.
   Leave a glass of water by the bedside
of the dying where the Angel can clean

   his sword and dry it after. Rain at a funeral
means good luck. Don't visit the same grave
   twice in one day. Leave a pebble on the stone
so the soul does not rise, follow you home.

Lines Written during a Pandemic

From the kitchen comes the soft,
regular sound of chopping,
my husband cutting up tomatoes
and cukes for our dinner.
Then the bright, digital *bloop*
as his phone's Bluetooth connects
to the speakers, KKCA's *smooth jazz*
like a breeze in the living room's
still air. Late sun filling my office,
and from outside, a car door
gently closed. Where could our
neighbor be going? We're all shut
in these days, "self-isolating"
and "social distancing," watching
the rising or flattening curves.
No farmer's market, no concerts
in the park, our local art-house theater
closed—oh, I could craft a litany
of what we can't do anymore, of what
is needed and what's been lost.
"Imagine all the awful coronavirus
poems," a friend says. In the video
our daughter-in-law texted us last night,
our grandson sits with his father,
who holds his phone before them.
They're singing Woody Guthrie—
This land is your land, this land is my land—

and I'm not thinking, forgive me,
of the dead and dying, or even
of my own fears that this is how
I'll end, alone in a hospital, unable
to speak or hear the nurses turning
me twice a day—instead, I watch
as A smiles, follows with a small finger
the lyrics crawling across the screen,
as if at four he could read them.
Each time he sings the word *your*,
he taps his father's chest.

Forced March

What would I have to be to speak about him . . .

—ADAM ZAGAJEWSKI

I

I remembered it wrong, the scene in the film
within the film about Radnóti—there were no young
lovers coming upon the killing in the woods.
It was an older man and a woman who might have
been his daughter. And the soldiers hustling
Radnóti and the other Jewish prisoners too weak
to work, and not dying fast enough, to dig
their own mass grave, then coolly shooting them
one by one, might have been their beloved sons
and grandsons. And I may have dreamed those listing
skeletons marched through postcard towns,
sunshine on rags, the apple sellers, a blonde child
rolling a wheel with a stick past the starving men.
The wide-angled views of lush and lovely country—
Hungary, Yugoslavia, Germany. Those tracking shots
of green swells of pasture and innocent cows
grazing, peasants carrying their ancestral hatreds
along with the sparse grain and potato crops
in mule-drawn carts. Those closeups of adolescent
soldiers grateful someone else is led away.
A cart man feeding fresh hay to his horses.
The autumn woods suffused with morning light.

2

Everywhere in Hungary there are statues of him—
in front of libraries, town halls. In the cover photo
of my new translation he's cast in bronze.
Slender and tall, he leans against a wooden rail
in a sunlit park, his handsome profile tilted down,
as if he's staring at his shoes, lines forming, perhaps,
in his mind. His poems were *prophetic*, writes one scholar,
his gift arising, she thinks, from his *Jewish predisposition
to anticipate the worst*. In the camps, on the marches,
he wrote. In his filthy bunk, among the worms and lice.

> *The poet writes, as dogs howl or cats mew.
> Or small fish coyly spawn. What else am I to do?*

3

For the denouement, the director's framed
the exhumation site: a row of pine coffins
lined up neatly as shipping crates,
on top of each a pile of rags, each man's
things roughly displayed for whoever is left
to claim them. On Radnóti's the famous raincoat,
hidden in the pockets, his photos and letters,
an exercise book of ten poems. Folded within
its pages, a flyer advertising cod-liver oil,
Radnóti's final lyric on the back. I can't stop

thinking of how he'd written, five times,
in five languages—*the French and English . . .*
rather blurred and party illegible—
on the book's first leaf, the same message—

> *Please, forward this booklet which contains the poems*
> *of the Hungarian poet Miklós Radnóti . . .*
> *Thank you in anticipation.*

After Reading the News this Morning,
I Turn to the Curses of My Ancestors

A Found Poem

May you live to a hundred and twenty,
without a head. May you grow
like an onion with your head in the ground.
May you crawl on your belly.
May you become swollen and veined
as a mountain, pepper in your nose
and salt in your eyes. May all your teeth
fall out, except one to give you a toothache.
May you have a hundred houses,
in each house a hundred rooms, in each
room twenty beds, and may fevers
and chills toss you from bed to bed to bed.

Dream Poem Beginning with
Three Lines from Stephen Dunn

Often a sweetness
has come and changed nothing in the world

except the way I stumbled through it,

but not last night,
when once again Nurse B

came to me. Even in my dream
I knew she wasn't really the Angel

of Death, just a poorly paid hospice temp
who liked to scare me—*Birds carry disease, girl,*

you'd better take care. Your cold could be that flu
come up from Haiti, paralyze you to stone—

and finish the chocolate kisses
that were Mom's last pleasure,

flirt with M. Just bad luck
it was her on first shift

that last morning. *I can smell the death*
from her mouth, she said to me,

I hate that smell of death. Still, could it be,
after all, some kind of *sweetness*

that she returns to me in my sleep,
that finally I can confess

I blamed her, knowing so little
of her life, for her rush to leave once

they'd carried Mom's body
away, covered, on a stretcher?

Does she come back so I can forgive
her for asking me, as I stood,

stunned with grief in my mother's kitchen,
if she could have Mom's car?

This Side

What are you doing on this side of the dark?

—MARY KARR

You'll be glad to know you still come to me daily.
This evening, for instance, you arrive
fixing your lunch in the small sunny kitchen
of your Florida condo. Dressed in one of your blowsy
flowered *muumuus* and frayed slippers,
you shuffle across the linoleum you still scrub,
yourself, at eighty. I'm watching as you lift
a slick glass jar of sauce, iced over with crystals,
from the freezer, set it in what you call *the micro*,
and slam the little door. Why, all my life,
did you slam every door you shut? *How much sauce
can I eat?* you explain, then sit to your pasta
and iced tea, CNN *too loud*, I scold, on the cheap
portable you keep for company on the counter.
You've ignored, again, my nagging—frozen glass?
oven mitts scorched black?—wise to my fears.
So this is how you come to me. I reach for a jar,
I cross the floor, watch the news on TV, and grief
seizes me again, and again your ghost's so vivid
it seems you must be still living, still hurrying,
as you did, even in old age, from room to room,
speaking love to the cockatoos you swear understand
you, and aloud to me, though I'm not there.

On Prospect

I wasn't spying, just idling
at the hotel's picture window

when I saw them, a slender boy
and girl dressed in jeans

and thin jackets I thought too slight
for January. They were walking

away from me, holding hands,
and even from nine stories up

I could see they were young.
And I watched as they stopped,

and he turned to her, lifted her arm,
and twirled her entirely around,

dancing right there beside the bare trees
and afternoon traffic on busy

Prospect; and they were lovely,
and I was glad when he leaned down

and kissed her upturned face.
It was, I thought, the kind of kiss

you see in glossy perfume ads
underscored by Louis Armstrong,

and I thought about all they could not
know and whether they would

last, as we have lasted, love, though
we couldn't have known forty

years ago we'd have such luck. Still,
we must have known something—

don't you think?—in those early days
when driving in your red Toyota

through the rush of Dallas traffic,
at every yellow light and stop sign,

you'd turn and lean so sweetly into me.
At every stop, that kiss.

Acknowledgments

My heartfelt thanks to the editors of the following publications in which these poems first appeared, sometimes in slightly different form or with different titles:

ABQinPrint: "Eleanor Can't Sleep"

American Journal of Poetry: "Charm against Recollection," "Western," "Michael Corleone Prepares for Bed," and "Hunger"

Blackbird: "After Reading the News this Morning, I Turn to the Curses of My Ancestors: A Found Poem," "Eleanor Remembers Her Soldier," and "Now That You're Nowhere"

Bosque: "First Light"

Cultural Daily: "From Her Chair in a Hoop of Pale-Yellow Lamplight" and "Poem Beginning with a Line from Adelia Prado"

Hole In The Head Review: "At the Chicago Art Institute," "Autobiographobia," "For Ruth Ellis, Last Woman Hanged in England," and "Sympathetic Magic"

I-70: "Childhood" and "Not One Woman I Know Hasn't These Stories"

James Dickey Review: "This Side"

Minyan: "On Reading That, According to the Jewish Calendar, Days Begin with Night"

Nine Mile: "On Prospect," "Postcard from New Hampshire," "Ode," and "This Morning My Friend Writes"

North American Review: "Shameeka," "Shift Reports: Skilled Care" (from "Three Rispetti"), and "*La Liseuse*"

Numero Cinq: "Jag" (from "Three Rispetti," published as "Lit"), "Tea Boys," and "The Television" (from "Three Rispetti")

On The Seawall: "A Walk with Frank O'Hara," "Monday," "Dish Pigs," and "In My Other Life My Mother Fails"

Plume: "The Beautiful American Word *Baby*" and "*Forced March*"

South Florida Poetry Journal: "Dream Poem Beginning with Three Lines from Stephen Dunn" and "The Worn-Out Dancing Shoes"

Summerset Review: "Jane County Corrections," "There but for Fortune," and "*People Knew How to Dress in the Forties*"

SWWIM: "Errata"

The Night Heron Barks: "Song" and "*only here. only now.*"

Many thanks to Denise Brady and Guy Duncan of Gibraltar Editions for publishing several of these poems as a beautiful limited-edition letterpress chapbook, *First Light*; to Lisa Fay Coutley for reprinting the three poems that comprise "Three Rispetti" in her wonderful anthology, *In the Tempered Dark: Contemporary Poets Transcending Elegy* (Black Warrior Press); and to Lynn Miller and John Modaff for featuring three of these poems on their terrific podcast, *The Unruly Muse*.

I am deeply grateful for the community of poets, editors, and readers whose friendship and support I can't imagine life without—too many to name here, but especially Erin Belieu, Greg Donovan, Denise Duhamel, Mary Flinn, Ben Furnish, Harvey Hix, Dave Jauss, Danny Lawless, Suzanne Lummis, Anna Monardo, Erin Murphy, Rachel Pastan, Ron Slate, Maura Stanton, Mary Helen Stefaniak, and David Wojahn. Most special thanks to Jan Freeman and Jody Stewart for our Monday swaps, to Betsy Sholl and Leslie Ullman for our August and Friday projects, and to my sister-from-another-mother, Carol-Lynn Marrazzo.

Heartfelt thanks to Hilda Raz, Elise McHugh, James Ayers, and everyone at the University of New Mexico Press for their support and care for my work. I'm honored to join the brilliant list of Mary Burritt Christiansen poets. Special thanks and much love to Michael David for allowing us to use his beautiful painting.

Finally, so much love and gratitude to Jeffrey Aizenberg and to all my family; you fill my life with joy and make this work, and everything else that matters, possible.

Notes

"The Beautiful American Word *Baby*" is after John Weir's "The Beautiful
   American Word 'Guy.'"
"Eleanor Remembers Her Soldier" is for Bob Churchill.
"In My Other Life My Mother Fails" is after Carl Dennis's "Two Lives."
"Errata" is after Gerald Stern's "Blue Skies, White Breasts, Green Trees."
The borrowed line in "Poem Beginning with a Line from Louis Simpson" is
   from Louis Simpson's "American Classic."
The borrowed line in "Poem Beginning with a Line from Adelia Prado" is
   from Adelia Prado's "Passion," translated by Ellen Watson.
"Postcard from New Hampshire is for Carol-Lynn Marrazzo.
"Autobiographophobia" is for David Jauss.
"On Your Wedding Day You Must Fast and Weep" makes use of curses and
   superstitions I discovered in *How to Avoid the Evil Eye*, by Brenda Z.
   Rosenbaum and Stuart Copans, as well as those passed down to me by
   my own grandmothers.
Some of the curses I use in "After Reading the News this Morning, I Turn
   to the Curses of My Ancestors: A Found Poem" can be found in
   Stutchkoff's *Der Oytser fun der Yidisher Shprak* on YiddishWit.com.
The borrowed lines in "Dream Poem Beginning with Three Lines from
   Stephen Dunn" are from Stephen Dunn's "Sweetness."
"On Prospect" is for Jeffrey Aizenberg.
"Childhood" is in memory of Edward Singer (1922–2001).
"First Light," "*People Knew How to Dress in the Forties*," and "Three Rispetti"
   are in memory of Edith Latman Singer (1927–2015).